Withered Rose Can Bloom Again

Overcoming Life's Pitfalls Through Faith

By Clintoria Session

A Withered Rose Can Bloom Again: Overcoming Life's Pitfalls Through Faith
First edition published in 2015 by Anointed Ink. Second Edition Published by Leading Through Living Community LLC

Copyright 2018 by Clintoria Session

ISBN-13: 978-0-9991308-9-6

Scripture quotations are from the Holy Bible, King James Version (KJV) - www.Bible.com

All Rights Reserved. No part or portion of this publication may be reproduced, stored in a retrieval system, or transmitted in any form or by any means - electronic, mechanical, photocopying, recording, or otherwise - without the express written consent of the author.

For information:
Leading Through Living Community LLC
6790 W. Broad Street Suite 300
Douglasville, GA 30134

DEDICATION

This book is dedicated to my mother, the late Brenda Wakefield. Mom, you taught me so much more than you ever realized. You were the epitome of what it meant to be a Proverbs 31 woman. Being a single parent, you had to wear many hats and I know you probably cried many tears in secret because the weight of the world was on your shoulders. You always wore a brave face and kept smiling. You opened your heart and home to those who were in need.

Mom, you taught me what it meant to love unselfishly and to have the faith of Job when faced with adversity. You never allowed the word "can't" to be spoken because you taught us that all things are possible with God. Thanks for giving us a solid faith based foundation. Your faith in God was amazing even through your battle with cancer. When you were fighting the biggest battle of your life, you still took the time to encourage others.

I remember one of the last conversations we had. You were in the hospital and the prognosis wasn't great, but you looked at my tear stained face and spoke these words that are forever etched in my heart: "Sister, no matter what, you always remember that we serve a mighty God." Yes mom, our God is mighty and He has been my anchor. I miss you more than words could ever express. You were my biggest cheerleader and made me feel like I could accomplish anything.

Mom, I hope that I am making you proud. Love you to pieces!

In memory of Charles O. Harrison: Uncle, father, friend. Love and miss you!

ACKNOWLEDGEMENT

Thank you God for choosing me to carry your word. You have been a constant friend and you have loved me unconditionally. You have never given up on me and continue to bless me with your grace and mercy. I am so grateful that you never see me in my present state, but you see what I am to become. Thank you for every blessing and help me to never take your love for granted.

To my husband Samuel Session, Jr., we have been on this journey together since high school. We've had our share of ups and downs, but our faith in God continues to sustain us. You always know what to say to get me to smile with your wit. I am grateful for your listening ear and praying spirit. You are a man after God's heart. I thank God that He created you just for me and I can't imagine my life without you.

To my three wonderful gifts, my sons Micah, Jamal, and Titus. I am so grateful that God chose me to be your mom. You guys never cease to amaze me with you genuine hearts, compassion for mankind, and love for God. There were times when I wasn't feeling well and you interceded on my behalf. You guys are old souls and I can't wait to see how God will use each of you to continue to impact this world. Continue to allow God to order your footsteps and never lose faith when faced with adversity.

Aunt Jeanette, you are a mom who lost a daughter, and I the daughter who lost a mom. God knew that we needed each other and I thank Him for the bond that we share. You have blessed my life more than you will ever know. You were always there to pray for me when I couldn't pray for myself. During the loss of my mom, you were there encouraging me to keep pressing and you reminded me that God was with me. You have accepted me just as I am and allowed me to bear my wounds without fear of being judged or talked about. I appreciate your prayers and Godly counsel. May God continue to bless you and I pray that your later years are your best years.

To my girlfriends: thank you for your transparency, encouragement, laughter, tears and prayers. We are our sister's keeper and I love each of you.

God has blessed my life with so many wonderful people. To Mattie Bell Webb, my aunts, uncles, cousins and in-laws: thank you for your guidance and support. To my brother Dushuan Caldwell: allow God to shape you into the man He created you to be. Walk towards destiny because there is greatness inside of you.

Last but not least, to my big brother, the late Minister Cornelious Harrison: your support and love meant the world to me. I wish you were here to share in this moment with me. I love you and miss you!

CONTENTS

Dedication	iii
Acknowledgement	v
Introduction	1
Chapter 1 The Base	3
Chapter 2 The Foundation	9
Chapter 3 The Transition	31
Chapter 4 The Children's Bread	51
Chapter 5 The Pouring Rain	59
Chapter 6 The Call	66
Chapter 7 Words to Live By	73

INTRODUCION

Bad things happen to good people, but God is able to heal and restore the broken hearted. We are never too far out of the reach of God's love.

It is my prayer that as you begin to read the words of this book that the spirit of God will begin to give you a deeper revelation of the things that you have encountered in your life, and that you will realize that your trials came not to make you weak, but to make you strong. Open your heart and mind to God.

Your life has purpose and you have the victory!

Chapter 1
THE BASE

Beep, beep, beep! *Slam!*

"UGH!!!" moaned Sabrina.

It can't be 6:00am again?! But thank God it's Friday and I am so looking forward to going away with my husband, Marcus, to Savannah for the weekend.

I laid in the bed for another 10 minutes; it seemed as though my covers had arms holding me down so I couldn't move. With images of sugar plums still dancing in my head, I managed to pull myself out of bed and get the kids ready for school.

I found the strength to get myself ready for what would be a day full of meetings. We had won a major account and I had meetings scheduled to discuss strategic planning. I dropped the kids off at school and made my way to the interstate to head to work.

Of course - bumper to bumper traffic! And today of all days! I need to be at work on time to prepare for my 9am meeting! Thankfully, traffic begin to move a little bit faster. Turned out a truck had lost a tire and luckily no one was injured.

I made it to the parking garage at work and nearly had to park on the upper deck. I sprint my way down to the elevator to enter into the building and said a bit breathlessly, "Good morning Linda, morning Susan, morning John."

Now that the morning niceties were out of the way, I made my way to my cubical, only to find a note attached to my monitor from Amy, the executive assistant to our CEO Mr. Kelly.

"Not today Lord," I said under my breath. But I guess I spoke it loud enough for Susan to hear me.

"What's wrong, Sabrina?" she asked.

"Mr. Kelly wants to see me in his office at 8:30 and this can't be good."

Mr. Kelly came from old money and his focus was more on numbers than people. He had a reputation for chewing people up and spitting them out.

"Sabrina, stop thinking the worst. Maybe you are getting promoted today. We all know you work hard and are very dedicated to the company."

I thought to myself in response, *Susan, thanks for your vote of confidence, but this is sure to be the best day of my career or I am about to be a statistic of the economy by becoming unemployed.*

Lord, could this be the day that my dream comes true? I could begin to hear my heart pounding inside my chest. I felt nauseous all of a sudden. My hands were now clammy and sweating. I could hear my mom's voice telling me to "trust God and walk in confidence". Mom had the faith of Abraham and always knew the right words to say. Gosh, how I miss that lady. When she was alive, I'd always call her in times like these, and she knew exactly what to say.

I made my way to the bathroom for one last check to make sure I didn't have any lipstick on my teeth and my hair was in place before I made my elevator ride to doom or destiny. *Jesus, please be with me and not let me say anything stupid during this meeting.*

I stepped on the elevator to ascend to the 10th floor of our office building. It seemed like we stopped on every floor between my second floor cubicle and the tenth floor suite. The closer we got, the louder my heart was beating and now I had a knot in my stomach. *Lord, I can't lose my job now.* We just purchased our dream home in the suburbs and my kids were in great schools. I had worked myself into a tizzy as my thoughts raced all over the place.

"Ding." The door opened to the tenth floor and it seemed as though my legs had become Jell-O. "Jesus, walk with me and don't let me fall," I kept repeating softly. Growing up, momma had instilled in me and my two brothers to always trust God and to lean on Him when we were weak. This was indeed one of the moments where I needed Him.

Come on Sabrina, get yourself together, God is with you were the words I kept repeating inside my head. Could this be the moment I had been waiting for? I have been with the company for five years and worked my way up to Junior Account Manager. Two months ago, I interviewed for a Senior Account Manager position which meant an annual salary increase of $30,000, an annual bonus, company car, and a corner office on the seventh floor. Lord, this would mean that I would no longer have to stress over money. What a blessing this would be to my family!

I stepped off the elevator and approached Amy's desk. Before I could utter a word, she smiled with her rosy cheeks and said, "Good morning Sabrina, I will let Mr. Kelly know you are here. Have a seat in the waiting area and he will be with you momentarily."

Yep, this can't be good. We have 2500 people in our company and the executive assistant whom I never personally met knows me by name. As I sat in the waiting room, I noticed a beautiful bouquet of red roses sitting on the coffee table next to me. They were so vibrant in color they almost looked artificial. I leaned closer to the beautiful crystal vase and experienced such a sweet aroma. Looking closer at them in appreciation, it was then I noticed that towards the back of what looked like three dozen blooms was one nestled in the bunch that had begun to wither.

How could this be? I thought to myself. How could these others be so vibrant and that one not? At that moment, I felt a shear calmness and peace. I started reflecting on my life and what all I had gone through to get to this moment and tears begin to well up in my eyes. I had once been like that lonely rose that was nestled amongst the vibrant ones. And as I sat there waiting for the final word on my dream job, my mind drifted back to my beginning…

Chapter 2
THE FOUNDATION

I grew up in a small town where the population was around 2,000 and everyone knew you or someone in your family. My grandmother worked at one of the schools and we called her "Big Mama". Big Mama was always bringing home the pint size milk that was given to her by Mrs. Crumpton, the head nutritionist at the school. From time to time, she would also bring home canisters of peanut butter. It was hard enough to play ball with, and if you didn't have about five pints of milk or a gallon of water to wash it down with, you were sure to choke.

Every Saturday we would make the 30-minute drive from our house in the country to "town". I always looked forward to getting a pack of the gum that resembled chewing tobacco, a handful of tootsie rolls or Mary Janes. Riding with Big Mama was always an adventure and she only knew one speed: FAST! One day we were driving into town and the closer we got to the red light, which was yellow, the faster she seemed to drive. All of a sudden, we came to a screeching halt as she slammed on the brakes trying not to run the light. Lord, somehow I ended up on the floorboard of the backseat of that old black Buick that seemed long as a football field.

When we got to town, it seemed like Big Mama knew everyone in the store because they would greet her by name, Martha. My Big Mama sure seemed to be popular and well-liked, but how could this be when she was so stern with us kids?! Big Mama didn't hold any punches and you never had to wonder what was on her mind because whatever came up was sure to come out; whether you were offended or not.

One day during one of our visits to Harper's Store, Mrs. Irene, who was one of the "holy mother's" at church, walked in and made a beeline to greet Big Mama.

"Well, hello Martha, how are you doing?"

You would think Big Mama would just give the basic greeting of "fine" and keep it moving, but nooooo, she had to go into detail of why we were in Harper's to buy me some castor oil because I hadn't been to the bathroom in a few days and when I go I have to strain to have a bowel movement!!! How embarrassed this made me feel! This was one of those moments when I wish I had special powers like the lady on *Bewitched* and could twinkle my nose and vanish. Now, everybody at church will know that I am constipated because folks at church seemed to call around and spread everybody's business over the phone! I couldn't wait to leave that store.

When we returned home from town, I ran as fast as I could inside the house trying to fight back my tears. Honestly, what six-year-old wants such personal business discussed out in the open for everyone to hear!? Way to go Big Mama!!

***

Every Saturday night, Big Mama always cooked hamburgers, french fries and made the best sweet tea!! Me, my brothers, and cousin would always eat while watching our Saturday line up of *WWE* wrestling with Ricky Steamboat, Rick Flair and the Junkyard Dog followed by everyone's favorite *Hee Haw*! My Pawpaw would be right there with us kids enjoying every episode and taking up for us when Big Mama would fuss about the television being too loud or us laughing too hard.

Pawpaw and Big Mama had been married for years and were my mother's parents. I don't know how Pawpaw and Big Mama met, but I guess when they say opposites attract, it had to be true because

Pawpaw was so nice and he never got caught up in the church's gossip mill. He would spend time with us kids fishing and riding in that old blue Chevy pick-up truck in the pasture to feed the cows. Pawpaw didn't like to argue and was always the peacemaker. However, he would take a sip every now and then and when he did, Big Mama was on his heels fussing.

***

My mom was a single parent, so me and my brothers would spend a lot of time at my grandparents during the weekends. My parents divorced when I was two years old, and I really don't have a memory of them ever being together because I was so young.

We didn't mind spending time down in the country at Big Mama's because it was always an adventure when we went outside to play. Being in the country, we had all of God's creation at our fingertips and used our imagination to create things to play. One of our favorite things to do was to skip rocks in the water. My brothers and cousin seemed to have it down pat. It took me a minute to catch on, but I wasn't about to let no smelly boys outdo me!

One day after a heavy rain, we raced outside to the pond and grabbed a handful of rocks. My brother said, "Sabrina, I don't know why you going to try because skipping rocks isn't for girls and you never get it right." Well, this made me mad and I was going to show him once and for all! As I lifted my rock, getting ready to glide it into the water, I looked up into the sky and there was the most beautiful rainbow I had ever laid eyes on. It was full of color and I knew this was the day that I would shut his mouth once and for all: God had just placed a rainbow in the sky just for me! I wound up my arm and released the rock into the water and it was as if the rock had legs and began to walk across the pond!!! My brother stood there with his mouth open, and for the first time ever he didn't have a smart comment to say.

I stood there in amazement myself, but of course I wasn't about to let him see it. From that day forward, he never said anything to me about skipping rocks because me and my rainbow silenced his trap – at least for a few minutes.

***

Sundays were always the highlight of our weekends because we would gather at Big Mama's for dinner. All of my cousins, aunts, uncles, and whoever was hungry would show up for a feast of sorts. But before you could eat, you had to make it through church service! We had two churches to choose from - either Big Mama's or Pawpaw's church. Most of the family attended Pawpaw's church because it had the most reasonable timing and you didn't have to pack a lunch.

Pastor Brown led Pawpaw's church, and he preached every Sunday. He seemed to have the same lineup and often ended his sermons using the same words. You always knew when it was time to go because he would end with the same song. This particular Sunday, the senior choir was up singing and my cousin Mike started laughing because it was obvious that somebody was off key — the person sounded like a cat in heat! My Aunt June happened to see my cousin's outburst and gave an eye to Sister Rose who then turned around and pinched Mike's leg so hard, I thought he was going to start howling and run for Pastor Brown's healing line.

Sister Rose was one of the old mothers of the church and all of us kids were afraid of her. She was much like Big Mama: mean. She also wore her glasses on the tip of her nose and smelled like moth balls.

As I looked around the church, I noticed all the women wearing white and there was a table in the front of the church draped with something that looked like a white sheet. It covered something on the table that protruded up as if there might be a body or something under there. My heart began to race. If we were in the church with a dead person, I was going to scream and didn't care how hard Sister Rose pinched me.

Pastor Brown was near the close of his sermon and then said we need to prepare ourselves for communion. The choir came down and sat in the audience, and all the old women started putting on white gloves. They marched up front and as they begin to remove that white sheet, my heart was pounding so fast that I almost lost my breath. I didn't know what to expect.

This was the first time I had been in the service where they had communion. I was usually in Mrs. Robinson's children's class, but she was out sick and all of us kids had to attend the boring big church that made absolutely no sense. It was very confusing why grown people would come to church and tell the entire congregation about their aches and pains, have Pastor Brown touch them, leading to them falling out on the floor. This was some scary stuff to me and I couldn't wait for Mrs. Robinson to get well.

The women removed the white sheet and there was some silver containers that held little cups of grape juice and there were trays of little white cookies. Pastor Brown begin to lead the church in singing a song about drinking the blood!!!! Lord, what in the world was this going on and who wants to drink somebody's blood?! I didn't know what Pastor Brown was talking about because then he started talking about eating the cracker, and that it was symbolic of Jesus' body and the juice was His blood. They passed the juice and crackers around, but us kids were not allowed to touch it which was fine by me because I was totally confused and ready to go!

Church was finally over with, and me and my brothers raced to get in momma's car to head to Big Mama's for some good eating and hours of fun! As we walked in the door, we smelled a mixture of aroma's coming from Big Mama's kitchen, with the smell of fried chicken overpowering everything. Momma and my aunts always sat at the table as Big Mama transferred all of her food from pots into nice dishes that were eventually placed on the table as well. This made no sense to me because it just meant twice as many dishes to wash, but it did make the table look really pretty. Man, all these smells made me so hungry. Finally, everyone had arrived and we could eat.

Big Mama must have been up all night cooking. She had turnip greens, green beans, a roast, fried chicken, corn bread, potato salad, macaroni and cheese, rice and gravy, yams, apple pie and to top it all off, my favorite - chocolate cake!!!!!! I couldn't wait to tear into all this goodness.

The adults sat around the big table, and us kids had a table in the den to eat because kids were not allowed in grown folks' conversation. It didn't matter to me because I didn't care to hear all that gossiping and besides, me and my nine cousins had a lot of catching up to do ourselves.

The food was so good and we all ate until our bellies expanded. After we had let our dinner digest for 30 minutes (some rule Big Mama set), me and all my cousins except for prissy Julie, ran outside to play a game of kickball. We had so much fun and stayed out there until it got dark and it was time to head home for another week of school.

***

Mondays were always hard because momma got us up super early at 6am to make sure we had breakfast and to make sure my brothers didn't miss the bus. I didn't ride the bus because I went to a school out of our zone and momma had to drop me off at Mrs. Smith's house every morning to walk with her across the street to the school. Mrs. Smith was a cook at the elementary school where I attended and momma knew her pretty well. She was a sweet ole lady who always looked out for me and made sure I was okay at school. On cake day, she always gave me an extra piece on my lunch tray.

It seemed that God always surrounded us with people who would look out for us. They must have known how hard it was for my momma to provide for me and my 2 brothers on her salary. Momma always talked about God and how He would always provide for His children. I guess that meant we were part of His family because people were always giving us stuff. For instance, Mrs. Alexander would send us bags of clothes that her granddaughter could no longer wear and most of the items looked like they had never been worn.

I loved recess time at school and couldn't wait to go meet my friends Jim, Michelle, Luke, Mary, and Paulette on the monkey bars and swings. The swings were my favorite. We would race to see who could reach the clouds. Although we knew none of us would, every day we tried harder and harder.

At the end of the school day, I walked to the babysitter's house with my friend Kim. Her big brother, Larry, was much older and was out of high school. He would walk to pick her up every day and I walked with them when Mrs. Smith had to stay late. The babysitter's house wasn't far from Kim's and most of the time, Kim stayed with us at Mrs. Lillie's. I loved going to Mrs. Lillie's because she had the best toys. Pretty much all the kids from school stayed there until their parents were off from work. Mrs. Lillie was like a second mom to me and I knew I was her favorite 'cause she would buy me things and carried me on vacations with her. None of the other kids got to do those things and I knew I was special to her. She and my mom were great friends as well and many times, she had dinner waiting when my mom would come to get me in the afternoons. Yep, we were definitely God's family!

The joy before the storm…

It was three days away from my eighth birthday and I couldn't wait!!!! Mom was allowing me to have a party and I got to invite all my cousins and some of the kids from church and school. My Uncle Jimmy and Aunt Rachel had asked me what I wanted for my birthday, and I told them I wanted a pool and a new bathing suit. They were my favorite and I often spent weekends with them when my mom needed a break. I liked going over to their house because we would always go out to eat on Saturdays, something we didn't do much at home because mom couldn't afford it.

The morning of my birthday, which happened to be a Saturday, Uncle Jimmy and Aunt Rachel came to carry me to town to pick out my present... And there it was, a pretty pink plastic pool with Cinderella plastered all over it!!!! It was my lucky day because they only had one left! My uncle grabbed it before anyone else did while me and Aunt Rachel made our way to the bathing suits. There had to have been hundreds to choose from in all colors, but I was looking for something in my favorite color purple.

After looking for what seemed to be an hour, we found the perfect one: a purple swimsuit with ruffles and a picture of Cinderella that matched my pool! I was soooo excited and couldn't wait to get back home to show mom!

When we got back to my house, mom, Big Mama and my Aunt Nellie had started to decorate the tables with balloons and streamers while Pawpaw and my two brothers fired up the grill for the hot dogs and hamburgers. This was going to be the best birthday ever and I couldn't wait for my friends to arrive to see my new pool and bathing suit.

One by one, they all came and soon my plastic pool was full with 8 kids splashing around. Uncle Jimmy had to use the water hose to refill the pool several times because we splashed out the water as soon as he filled it up. I couldn't believe all these people were here to celebrate ME; I felt like a princess! Mom had even invited Mrs. Lillie and Mrs. Smith who showed up with gifts!

After about an hour in the pool, we all begin to look like raisins in the sun and it was time to get out and eat. The hamburgers were bigger than my mouth and all the kids seemed to enjoy them. As I looked across the table, my friend Kim had mayonnaise plastered across her mouth as she was trying to eat the whopper of a hamburger, while Tommy was on his second; he sure could eat.
At lunch he was always the one eating everybody's leftovers. You would have never known he ate that much because he was skinny as a rail.

It was time for cake and singing "Happy Birthday". Big Mama went into the house and walked out with her specialty: a seven-layer chocolate cake! YUMMY! My friends were about to taste a little bit of heaven. Big Mama could give Betty Crocker a run for her money! She was always baking cakes and pies for the church and for people in the community. Momma placed eight pink candles on the cake and all the kids gathered around the table as momma led everyone in singing "Happy Birthday". At the end of the singing, I took a deep breath, closed my eyes to make a wish, and with one puff, blew out the candles! Momma cut all the kids a slice of cake while Big Mama gave everyone a scoop of Pawpaw's homemade vanilla ice cream. We all were eating cake and ice cream when out the corner of my eye, I caught a glimpse of old Susie Westmoreland walking in the yard crashing my party.

Susie was my friend Jamie's older sister and she gave me the creeps. There was just something about Susie that made my stomach churn at her presence. She didn't say very much, but she would just stare at you as if you were an alien or something. Susie was 16 and could drive, so her mom sent her to pick up Jamie from the party. *Lord, please let Jamie hurry up and wolf down that cake and ice cream so he can leave with ole creepy Susie*, I thought to myself.

"Susie, please sit down and have some cake with us," mom said to my internal objections. Luckily, she and Jamie were in a hurry because they had to go to the grocery store to pick up a few items that their mom was waiting on. They left and I could get back to enjoying my party.

After everyone finished eating, I opened my gifts. My friend Alison and Amanda, who were twins, gave me a pretty ballerina jewelry box that played music each time you opened it. They always gave nice gifts because their mom worked at Roses Department Store and she got things really cheap. Momma saved her gift for last and as I opened the big box, I couldn't believe my eyes: my very own cabbage patch doll that was dressed in a yellow blouse, plaid skirt, and white shoes. She was the same color as I was and had two ponytails with red ribbons just like momma liked to fix my hair! I named her Miranda Marissa!

This was the best birthday ever and I didn't want it to end, but it started getting dark and my friends had to leave. Normally I would be sad to see everyone go, but not this time; I had Miranda Marissa to keep me company.

It was time to go to bed, and Miranda Marissa and I were curled up underneath the covers as momma walked in to give me her normal kiss on the forehead and to tell me that she loved me. This particular night, I grabbed her neck and squeezed her extra tight because this was the best birthday ever!

"Good night, 'Brina," she said. Momma was the only person who called me 'Brina but it was okay because I liked it. As I laid in the bed, I couldn't go to sleep without saying my prayers. Momma always told us to count our blessings each night and I had plenty to count tonight!

Everything Changed

My friend Jamie's birthday was two days after mine in June. He invited me to his party and while I was excited to go and play with my friends, I was dreading seeing ole creepy Susie. Jamie's mom and my mom were good friends and we all went to church together. Mom dropped me off at Jamie's for the party and when I walked in the backyard, I couldn't believe it: his uncle had brought one of his ponies for us to ride! She had the shiniest coat you every saw with one speckle of white on her nose. Jamie had a large yard so there was plenty of room to ride the pony. As we took turns riding, others were playing on the swing and seesaw. I was having fun plus I didn't see creepy Susie and hoped that she was gone somewhere far away.

I had been drinking a lot of soda and had to go to the restroom. Mrs. Lewis, Jamie's mom, showed me to the restroom and left me in the house while she went back outside. I closed the door and was beginning to pull my shorts down when in walks creepy Susie. My heart started racing out of my chest. What was she doing just barging in the restroom on people! Before I could say a word, she locked the door and told me not to say a word, and if I did, I would be very sorry.

I was scared because Susie was 16 and athletic. She was the captain on the girls' basketball team and she played ball as good as any boy. Here I was a little 8-year-old kid. How could I take on a 16-year-old? It was impossible. I tried to pull up my shorts but Susie stopped me. She told me she was going to make me feel good and make a woman out of me. *How was she going to make a woman out of an 8-year-old?* I thought.

She forced me to lay down on the bathroom floor. I was now beyond scared and didn't know what was going to happen to me. She pulled my legs apart and I was trying to kick her, but she had me pinned with her legs. She began to move her finger up and down on my private part and then she put her finger inside of me and begin to move her finger in and out. I was wiggling on the floor trying to get away from her and tried telling her to stop, but she placed her free hand over my mouth and said that she knew I liked it. Big tears were welling up in my eyes and I was confused and didn't know why she was doing this to me. She finally stopped when she heard someone walking in the hallway. I was too scared to move. Susie told me never to tell anyone because she would get in trouble and that our moms were friends and we didn't want them getting into it with each other. I wanted her to shut her stupid face up and get away from me.

Finally, she was gone and I was trying to get up from the floor. My legs were weak and my stomach was in a big knot. I wanted my momma bad. I sat on the toilet to pee and as I wiped, I had a spot of blood on the tissue. I was really scared now and the tears begin to flow. I don't know how long I was in the bathroom, but it must have been a long time because Jamie's mom came and knocked on the door to make sure I was okay. I told her I was. I tried hard to stop crying because I didn't want the other kids to ask me questions. As I walked out the bathroom door, there stood creepy Susie in the hallway and I ran past her so fast you would have thought something was chasing me. I went back outside and tried to play, but all I could think about was what just happened. I didn't understand any of it, all I knew was that my private area was sore and it hurt when I walked.

My stomach was still in a knot and it was all I could do to not burst out in tears. I finally told Jamie's mom I wasn't feeling well and asked her to call my momma to come and get me. It seemed like it took momma a long time to get there, but when she pulled up, I ran and hugged around her waist and started crying. She and Jamie's mom thought I must have gotten a virus and I didn't tell them any different because I had remembered what Susie said about them getting mad at each other.

We got in the car and on the way home momma stopped at the store and got me a Ginger Ale because she thought that would help my stomach. If only she knew what really happened. Momma was a good Christian lady and taught Sunday School, but if she knew what Susie did to me, she would have killed her and I couldn't risk momma getting into trouble. Heaven forbid if one of my brothers found out: Susie would be dead meat! I couldn't risk telling anyone because momma was all we had and I didn't want to do anything to cause her any problems.

It seemed like it took us two hours to get home. The whole time I stared out the window and the image of what happened to me kept replaying over and over. When I got home, I went straight to my room and got in the bed with Miranda Marissa and pulled the covers over my head trying to forget what just happened… but I couldn't. Every time I closed my eyes, I saw Susie looking at me as she slid her fingers inside me. I could still smell her stinking onion breath. She must have put a whole onion on her hotdog. I don't know why she did this to me. What did I do? Maybe I should have held my pee until I got home. Momma always said that Jesus would take care of us, but he must have been on vacation today because I was all alone in that bathroom. One thing is for sure, what happened wasn't right and I couldn't tell anybody but Jesus and Miranda Marissa.

At night when it was time to go to bed, I always heard momma talking to Jesus and she would always say, *Lord, you know it all and I am glad I can tell you anything.* I didn't really understand all that Jesus stuff, but I was pretty sure he could keep a secret.

Momma came in the room later on to check on me and to bring me some Ginger Ale, but I pretended like I was asleep so I wouldn't have to talk to her. I was never good at lying to momma and she could see straight through me so I figured I had better act like I was sleeping if I didn't want to play "Twenty Questions".

That had to be longest night. Seemed like it took me forever to go to sleep, and every time I closed my eyes, I relived what happened. I laid in bed staring at the ceiling as tears rolled down my cheeks. My pillow was soaked with tears and the knot in my stomach hurt really bad. One thing was for certain, I couldn't tell anyone what happened to me.

***

"Brina, time to get up," I heard my mom say. I couldn't believe it: I made it through the night and must have fallen asleep at some point.

I got up and had to pee so bad, but was scared because I didn't know if it would hurt or if I would have blood. I couldn't hold it any longer and went to the bathroom. I held my breath as I eased on the toilet and it only stung a little bit and I didn't see any blood when I wiped. I was really happy because my Sunday School class was going on our annual picnic to the state park today and I wanted to be able to have fun with my friends from church.

As I opened the door to exit the bathroom, I could smell bacon cooking. Mom had prepared us a big breakfast of bacon, eggs, grits and pancakes. She wanted to make sure our bellies were full before we left because we weren't scheduled to eat until 1pm at the park. Me and my brothers woofed down our food so that we could get ready to go. I couldn't wait to get to the park to ride the paddle boats. Last year, me and mom shared a boat and we must have stayed on the lake for four hours in that thing talking about whatever came to mind. I enjoyed when it was just me and mom because we had the best time laughing, talking and acting silly.

"Brina, you need to hurry up and put your clothes on so we can get ahead of the traffic," I heard mom say.

I raced to my room and put on the new outfit that my aunt had bought me. It was my favorite color purple with pink bows on the sleeves and legs of the shorts. She also got me purple socks to match and some pink tennis shoes. Mom had already combed my hair in a ponytail and tied it with a pink ribbon. I was ready to go.

My brothers were dressed and waiting on me. We all jumped in mom's green Cutlass and off we went to have a day of fun with friends from church. My mind was not on what happened to me at the party, but that day stuck with me forever.

Chapter 3
THE TRANSITION

Today was the last day of school before Spring break and I couldn't wait to hear the bell ring because my eighth grade band class was going to Washington on a field trip. We had raised money by selling fruit to go and I couldn't believe that mom had agreed to allow me to travel that far away without any family chaperoning me. She was very protective of me since I was the only girl.

Mom had become like my big sister. She and I would talk for hours and I really enjoyed spending time with her. However, I was looking forward to being with my friends for four straight days as we visited the various sites in Washington.

During the bus ride, some of the chaperones were flirting with the some of the "more advanced" girls on the bus. One of the male chaperones named Tommy was very attractive. He had arms of steel, a smile that could light up a room, perfect white teeth and beautiful brown eyes. Obviously, Tommy didn't care that most of the girls on the bus were either 14 or 15 because he kept flirting. One of the girls, Sharon, who was known to be sexually active started pulling up her skirt making it shorter to reveal her thighs. Sharon was very popular in school with the boys as well as the girls. She was very pretty and curvy. She came from money and had long curly black hair. Sharon always got invited to everyone's party and wore the latest styles, so it wasn't a surprise to me that Tommy found her to be appealing. Unlike me, a plain Jane who wasn't allowed to wear make-up and whose clothes were always two fashion seasons behind. I could never attract someone like Tommy. I had the brains, but Sharon had the beauty.

After eight hours on the bus, we finally made it to Washington and pulled up to our hotel. Our teacher began to distribute the room keys and informed us of who our roommates would be. I was going to be with Alice, Missy and .... SHARON! Alice was a homebody just like me, Missy was a know it all, and SHARON was as hot as a firecracker! What a mixture in one room for four days.

As we entered the room, Alice and I decided that we would share beds and that left Missy to share with Sharon. We started unpacking our things and a box of condoms fell out of Sharon's suitcase! What in the world was she doing with condoms at the age of 15?! Missy hurried over to where she stood and began to ask her questions, all of which I wanted to hear the answers to. Come to find out, her mom had purchased them for her because she said she would rather for her to be safe than to wound up pregnant or with an STD! Now I realized why she was so promiscuous. Her parents were not teaching her what it meant to abstain and practically made it easy for her to have sex.

Sharon couldn't believe how we all were responding to her having condoms. She thought we were all a bunch of uptight church girls who were completely boring. She made it a point to tell us that she would be sneaking out of the room tonight to meet Tommy. We all tried to tell her that was wrong, but she didn't want to hear it and had made up her mind.

It was time for us to meet back at the buses to go to dinner. Me, Missy, and Alice all began to whisper and talk amongst ourselves about how loose Sharon was and how she would be the first one of us to have kids. As we got on the bus, Sharon sat in the seat across from Tommy and all they did the whole time was flirt with each other.

Tommy was 19 years old and was supposed to be a chaperone, but it seemed that he had other things on his mind. If Ms. Wilson found out what was going on, Tommy would be finding another way back home and Sharon would be expelled from school. However, we couldn't tell on them because then we would be seen as snitches. I already wasn't the most popular person in the world and was pretty much seen as the church girl, so I knew I wasn't going to say anything.

As we finished our meal, Mrs. Wilson informed us that lights had to be out and doors locked by 11pm because we had to board the bus the next morning by 8am to travel to the monuments. We made it back to the hotel and changed into our swimsuits because we had planned to meet as a group by the pool that night. I was so self-conscious because my boobs were larger than most girls in my class, my legs were like pencils, and my self-image was not very positive. It seemed like when I experienced that incident with creepy Susie, something on the inside of me changed. I started feeling like I wasn't good enough. My friends would tell me that I was too hard on myself, but they didn't know my secret and the torment that I lived with since that dreaded day.

While everyone else had on their two piece suits, Alice and I were the only ones wearing a one piece with a cover up. We had so much fun that night. Laughing and splashing water on each other and talking. For the first time in a long time, I felt like I fit in; I didn't feel awkward or less than.

As the night came to a close, it was time to go back to the room for bed. As Alice, Missy, and I got ready for bed, Sharon was getting all dolled up to meet Tommy. I couldn't believe that she was actually going to go through with meeting him. Wasn't she afraid of what would happen? What if she got caught? We tried to talk her out of it, but she told us to mind our business and to take our boring selves to sleep. She left out of the room around 11:15pm, after Ms. Wilson completed her room checks. Sharon said Tommy told her to meet him in his room to talk. Now what 19-year-old boy wants to "talk" to a 15-year-old girl?! Sharon knew what was going to happen because she carried some condoms with her.

When she left the room, Alice, Missy and I talked about how sad it was that she didn't value her body and how we couldn't imagine having sex at such a young age. As we continued to talk, my mind began to flashback to the day that my innocence was stolen from me and how painful it felt. If sex felt anything like that then I didn't want any part of it.

We talked until we must have drifted off to sleep. It was 2am when we heard a knock on the door. We all debated on who would get up to answer it. Missy was the brave one. Before she could ask who was it, we heard Sharon whispering to let her in. As she came through the door, her hair looked like she had been in a cat fight. She went straight to the shower and we all laid there waiting to hear what happened. Sharon emerged from the bathroom and begin to brag about how Tommy made her feel like a woman. She went into detail about how his penis was the largest she'd ever had and how he kissed on her vagina before they had sex. This was stuff that I had never heard of before, but I wasn't about to act like it. She said that Tommy was so experienced and that he told her that he loved being with her. He tried to get her to try anal sex, but she was afraid it would hurt too bad. Sharon was beside herself with excitement and I couldn't believe what I was hearing. Mom had always told me that I should wait until I got married to have sex and I wasn't in any hurry.

Every night that we were in Washington, Sharon met up with Tommy to continue their encounters. She returned to the room excited every night except for the last night. This particular night, she returned about an hour earlier than normal and was in tears. She went into the shower and seemed to stay in there forever. When she came out, she was crying. I was scared and didn't know what had happened to her. Sharon begin to tell us that the night started as normal with Tommy kissing her vagina and her kissing his penis. Once they were both "heated", Tommy put on a condom and they were having some pretty rough sex which they both enjoyed. She said when they had finished having sex and he withdrew his penis from inside of her, they realized that the condom had broken. She began to cry like a baby and played the "what if I'm pregnant game" all night long. Part of me felt pity for her and the other part of me felt like she had it coming to her for being so loose. None of us knew what to say so we said nothing except for me praying for her and then going to sleep.

The next morning, we boarded the bus to head home. For the first time on the trip, Sharon was quiet and sat at the front of the bus while Tommy sat at the back. I couldn't help but to feel sad for her because what eighth grader is ready to be a parent? I hoped she wasn't pregnant.

During the bus ride back home, I begin to think about my life, and although I wasn't popular, at least I didn't have to worry whether or not I was pregnant.

As we arrived back at school, mom was waiting on me. I was so ready to sit-up with her all night telling her all that I had experienced and seen; except of course for what Sharon had shared. Mom sat-up with me and listened as I rambled on and on about my adventure in Washington… but some things I didn't want to share…

When the earth shook

Mom had her annual doctor's appointment and afterwards we were going to the mall. I sat home waiting for her to come home and it seemed to take forever. Me and my brothers were watching television when Aunt Louise knocked on the door. I opened it to let her in and told her that mom was at the doctor's office for her annual checkup. She interjected and told me that mom had sent her to get us because the doctor had admitted her into the hospital for further testing.

My heart sunk into the bottom of my feet. Nothing could happen to my mom because she was the only parent I could count on. Who would take care of us? She was my best friend and I couldn't understand why God was allowing this to happen. I began to cry. My Aunt hugged me and told me not to overreact, and that mom was going to be okay.

My brothers had tears streaming down their faces, too, because they knew mom was all we had.

Aunt Louise drove us to the hospital to see mom, and as we walked into her room, I burst out crying to see her laying in that hospital bed. My brothers were trying to be strong, but they couldn't hold in their tears either. Aunt Louise had her arms around them as mom was comforting me. Me and my brothers began to ask what was wrong with her and the look on her face was an indicator that it wasn't good. She began to tell us that she had found a knot in her left breast a few weeks ago and she went to the doctor for testing. They called her in today to tell her that she had breast cancer and would need to have a mastectomy! I couldn't believe what I was hearing. How could this be and why was it happening to my mom? Doesn't God know that I am only 15 and that I need my mom?! Wasn't it enough that I had endured my violation??? Now my mom was in the fight of her life!

Me and my brothers couldn't stop crying. Mom and Aunt Louise did their best to assure us that everything was going to be okay, but it was hard to see past this present moment.

We were going to stay with Aunt Louise while mom was in the hospital. She was scheduled to have surgery in the morning and if everything went well, she would be home 24 hours after the surgery. I didn't want to leave mom's side that night because I was afraid I wouldn't see her alive again. She began to tell us to have faith and believe that God was a healer and that He was going to see her through this issue. Mom was such a strong believer and an encourager, but I really didn't want to hear anything about God at that moment. I didn't understand how God allowed so many bad things to happen to good people. Mom was the best one out of our family. She was so giving and always helped those in need. We didn't have an abundance of material stuff, but we had love. Mom always made sure that we knew we were loved, and that family and God were important. This just didn't make any sense to me.

It was getting late, so mom told Aunt Louise to take us home. I didn't want to leave her side, but she said she needed to rest for her surgery tomorrow. Before we left that night, we all joined hands and Aunt Louise prayed that God would be with mom through the surgery and that He would heal her body. Me and my brothers hugged mom and she promised us that she would be okay. She was so strong, yet I knew she had to be a little afraid.

That had to be the longest night of my life. As I laid in the bed, I kept hearing mom say that God was with her and that He would take care of her. I tried hard to believe those words, but where was God when Susie hurt me? Tears soaked my pillow; I was so confused and scared. I prayed hard that night that God not let my mom die and that He would do exactly what mom said He would do.

The next morning, Aunt Louise drove us to school and that afternoon, she would take us to see mom. All that day at school, all I could think about was my mom being in surgery and not knowing if she was alive or not. At lunch, I sat at the table with Alice and Missy. They asked me why I was sad and I told them what was going on. They told me they were sorry and tried to cheer me up, but that was impossible that day.

I noticed that Sharon hadn't been around in a few weeks and asked Missy if she knew where she was. She told us that Sharon was on homebound because she was pregnant with Tommy's baby! Oh my God, could my life get any crazier! Apparently, Sharon found out she was pregnant shortly after returning from the Washington trip and her parents thought that it would be best for her not to return to school because of the embarrassment. My brain felt like it was going to explode from all of the chaos around me.

Little Peace

As worried as I was, momma survived the surgery. We went to go see her directly after school and she was still her strong self. I was worried to see her there, but I was so grateful that she was alive and still with me. I was grateful that God answered my prayer and kept my mother safe while she was in surgery. She had the mastectomy and seemed to have the same spirit, even though she didn't look the same.

Over the next few weeks I was worried about the cancer coming back, but momma remained in remission. That made me even more grateful to have her there with me.

The summer ended and I entered into high school. I was overwhelmed with how different everything was and how big the building seemed. High school was very tough for me. I found myself fighting to fit in. I never felt like I belonged and I never felt that I was good enough. I attempted to hang out with the rest of the kids, after school and at parties, but I always felt so awkward and out of place. I was a wall flower and couldn't find my space in the "scene".

As I grew as a teen, I found that the molestation affected me more than I had realized. I found myself damaged emotionally and couldn't handle common life experiences. I often blamed myself for what Susie did to me because I couldn't understand why a person would just do that sort of thing without being provoked. I suffered greatly with low self-esteem and self-hatred. I felt dirty and unworthy of being alive at times. It was such a struggle to even get out of bed sometimes, but I felt that my only option was to keep it to myself. I was embarrassed and ashamed of what I had endured; I felt alone and isolated.

On top of my internal battle, I found myself battling with my sexuality. I wasn't sure if I liked boys or girls. I knew it was right to like boys, but something inside of me pulled my mind towards girls. It was like I was fighting myself every day of my life. The burden of this secret weighed me down in almost every area of my life. I found myself no longer interested in the things that I once liked and I couldn't get excited about things that were presented to me in school.

Despite how difficult everyday life was, I met a guy named Marcus. I didn't expect to meet someone in the midst of my storm, but Marcus seemed to come out of nowhere and peak my interest. I did the best I could to push down my secret and hide my feeble emotions, but there was something about Marcus that made me believe that he would someday be my husband.

I felt conflicted and frustrated at times, because as much as I liked Marcus, I still felt the pull on my sexuality. It made my days even more difficult to endure. I found myself going through the motions of life and not really being a participant. I went through the school day like a zombie and I came home to retreat from the world in a shell like a turtle.

I did not really know which way I was going. No matter how hard I tried, I realized that I was simply lost in my own life and my own pain. I suffered daily, yet I continued. I wasn't quite sure how or why I kept going, but I did. It was like there was something in me that kept breathing while the surface of me wanted to give up. There was constantly a battle raging within me and I didn't know if I would make it out alive.

As I entered my junior year of high school, I found that I learned how to wear my mask. I was able to hide my emotions fairly well and proceed about my day without feeling like the entire world was caving in on me. I began to get closer to Marcus and found myself liking him more. However, there was still that underlying thought of liking the same sex. It was like I could not shake it nor run from it. It felt like it was trying to take me over, but by no means would I let it. I knew where it came from and I knew the reason behind it; I just couldn't escape it.

Even though days seemed hopeless at times, I found some joy in some of the simple things in life.

And then it happened.

My father passed away.

My father was a severe alcoholic and ultimately the alcohol killed him. The pain of his death slithered its way into the hole where the rest of my pain lay trapped. I felt like I missed the boat, like I was on the outside of my own life.

It was hard to bury my father; I worried about his soul. I wasn't sure exactly why I was so concerned about his soul, especially when I did not fully understand what heaven and hell was, but I found myself begging God to tell me if he made it into heaven. I prayed as hard as I could and I asked God with my entire heart if my father made it to Him. I spent so much time asking that I almost missed the answer.

God eventually revealed to me that my father did make it in and that offered me great relief. I wasn't quite sure if my dad had a relationship with God, but who was I to say one way or the other. What I did know is that God had the final say on all that and I was in no position to question Him.

***

High school had its ups and downs (mostly downs), but I always felt that push to keep going. It was during this time that I discovered Christ for myself. I knew who God was because of my mother's relationship with Him, but in the back of mind I felt there was something that didn't line up. Then one day that changed. It wasn't some huge event, but rather the events leading up to that point in my life. I realized that even during every dark time that I had experienced, God called me. I could feel Him near me, even when I felt alone. It was with that realization that I received Christ into my life. From there, it seemed that everything changed and shifted in a completely different direction.

As I pushed to make it through the rest of my High School career, Marcus became one of the few people that I had grown to count on. He was a great friend to me and was there during some of the darkest times. He became a person that I could trust and rely upon, even when I was haunted by the ghosts of my past.

Marcus and I were attached to the hip all through high school. I looked to him to be my rock and he cared for me as I felt God chose me to be cared for. He made me feel safe and while I was growing with God, I felt that he was the one that God sent to keep me safe for the rest of my life. High school ended and Marcus and I got married.

I was 21 years old when one day I found myself thanking God for sustaining me through it all. I had endured many heartaches, but I found the love of God through Marcus, surviving high school, and making it to see my twenty-first birthday. But while I was grateful and truly blessed to marry Marcus, I realized my past was still an issue. I found it difficult to fully give myself to my husband sexually. What happened to me when I was a child damaged me in ways that I didn't even realize. I had a loving husband and a God that was faithful, but I was still broken and distant.

Over time, I confided in my husband about what happened. I was nervous and scared about what he would think of me, but I found that once I told him, I felt like a little bit of the weight was taken off. When I told him, he didn't know what to do or say to me, but I knew that he was trying his best to be understanding.

Even though I felt free after I told my husband, the nightmares still continued. I knew this was the enemy's way of keeping me bound to my past and keeping my husband and I sexually separated. I felt tormented and discouraged by what I was reliving everyday. The yoke of what happened to me was so heavy on me. The shame, pain, and anger would fight me each day. To top it off, I felt trapped because I would never get the opportunity to confront the abuser because she was deceased. I felt angry that I would never get to confront her, but also disappointed that she got away with what she did to me. I felt that she took the easy way out by dying. I felt cheated and left behind. There was a part of me that wanted her to pay and feel what she made me feel that day. I was angry and hurt all at the same time.

Despite my pain, Marcus and I were blessed with our first child. He was a joy and such a beauty in my eyes. We were excited to be parents, especially at such a young age. We would have the energy to keep up with our children, and hopefully live to see our grands!

Chapter 4
THE CHILDREN'S BREAD

Just when it seemed like everything was perfect, my child, whom I loved dearly, was diagnosed with a disability. My flesh was weak, but my spirit knew what to do. I was devastated and had a very difficult time accepting the hand I was being dealt. This was a time when all of me had to lean on God. My faith was all I had and trust was all God was telling me to do. I had no choice but to lean on Him. Despite what the doctors said, I had to trust God.

I spent many nights crying tears that I never thought I would cry. The pressure of life and the pressure of helping my son along was beginning to crush me. Pieces of me wanted to trust God, but my flesh was focused on all that I saw instead of all that God said.

The Background

I was two weeks overdue with my son and the doctor decided to induce me. After 22 hours of labor, it was discovered that he was posterior (face up instead of down). The doctor decided to turn him vaginally and when I began to push, he became logged in my pelvis. The doctor had to use forceps to pull my son out. He was born with the umbilical cord wrapped around his neck and he lost oxygen. He remained hospitalized for two days for observation to make sure everything was okay. And he was. He was my bundle of joy and was a very active little boy.

Too active.

When my son was five years old, he was diagnosed with Attention Deficit Hyperactivity Disorder (ADHD) and required medication. I fought it. I prayed hard for God to instantly heal my child because I never believed in medicating children, but he began to struggle so badly in school, so I reluctantly agreed.

The medication was a nightmare. My son became withdrawn and developed a tick. I prayed even harder for healing. I felt like a failure as a parent because I couldn't fix my child. I felt helpless and out of control of my life. We tried several different medications to address his illness, but they came with horrible side effects.
One day as I was walking into my job, God spoke to me. He said that the medication is what my son

needed for the moment and I had to continue trusting Him. My baby was in His hands. This gave me peace like nothing else.

I worked about 30 minutes from my home in a separate city from where my children attended school. One day while on the job, I received a phone call to say that my son had gotten into the medicine cabinet at his daycare, took several of his pills, and was being rushed to the hospital. My heart almost stopped.

I dashed to my car and made it to the hospital to see my five-year-old son in a zombie-like state. He was scared, but calm. I was relieved and angry. I doubted myself once again about whether I had made the right decision by placing him on medication. I prayed and God once again gave me peace.

When my son was seven, the school called me for a meeting and said they believed there was something wrong with him. He wasn't processing things the way the other children did. The school suggested that I allow them to test him. I reluctantly agreed to allow the testing and the results were that he had a severe learning disability. I didn't buy into what the school district was saying because they were famous for wanting to place labels on children. I wouldn't allow my son to be labeled as anything other than what God created him to be.

I took my son to a specialist to have my own testing completed, and while I was sitting there in the waiting room, there were moms with kids who were severely handicapped. Kids who couldn't contain themselves, and others who had to wear helmets because they would bang their heads on the wall. It was heartbreaking to see the different levels of disabilities; some that I had never seen before. My heart ached for the moms and what they must have been going through. Some were hurting so bad they couldn't hide it; it was truly written all over their faces.

As I sat there looking around, my eyes came back to rest on my sweet boy sitting beside me. It was as if God was saying, "Stop complaining and worrying. These parents have it much worse than you. You know me, so why don't you trust me?" Tears formed in my eyes and a strong sense of peace came over me.

My son's name was called and we went through several levels of tests. The results came back that he had mild brain retardation. The doctor sat there and told me that my son would never be able to comprehend doing basic things like making his bed, taking care of himself, play team sports, and all kinds of other things. It was a parent's nightmare.

But while the doctor was telling me all of the things my son would never do, I heard a small voice say "trust me." My baby looked at me, not really understanding or caring what the doctor was saying, and hugged me. I think he may have heard that voice, too!

On the drive home, all I could do was think about those other parents and the struggles they faced, and how I didn't understand what was going on and why God chose my son to endure what would be a lifetime of challenges... but we would make it through together.

I never disclosed to the school the results of my own testing because I didn't want my son to be labeled as anything negative. Each year he had an Individualized Education Program (IEP), and he struggled academically at times. But we never allowed him to say that he couldn't do something, and we didn't treat him any differently because of his struggles.

We decided to try team sports and enrolled our sin in soccer. WOW, how he excelled! He went on to play baseball and basketball; excelled there as well. All this contrary to what the doctor had said.

No one outside of my husband and best friend knew what the prognosis was for my son. I didn't need the negativity, nor people's opinions. If I was going to stand on God's promise, then I didn't need to give the enemy any ground by using the people around me.

When my son was in 5th grade, I had an educator tell me that he would never walk across the stage to obtain his diploma because of his learning disability. I discussed this with my husband and we began to research other schools. We decided to relocate to another county which had the resources that would benefit my son the most and better prepare him for life. It was tough moving away from my family, but this was the right decision to give him a chance at LIFE and it was the best decision we EVER made. The school's program was phenomenal and we saw such growth in our son. For once, we had a team of educators who believed and spoke life and possibilities into him.

He participated in sports and played varsity football. Our boy was very independent, but still performed under his grade level. Yet it was so much more than what we were told he would ever be able to do.

During our son's junior and senior years of high school, he participated in the job shadowing program and LOVED it. They loved him, too. Another major milestone his first doctor and old teacher said would never happen.

Ever since he was little, my son always had a heart for the underdog and looked out for that person. He has a heart of gold and never sees anything but the good in people. He has taught me so much through his perseverance. He realized through his academic years that he struggled, but he didn't allow that to stop him from trying.

During his senior year, we were coming from the store and talked about his struggles. I asked him if he ever wondered why he had difficulty processing things and he said "not really, mom." I told him the story about him losing oxygen at birth and we didn't realize until later that it had caused some damage to the part of his brain. He told me that he wasn't worried about it, that God made everyone different and that God had a plan. Here my son was schooling me when I was trying to teach him. I was very proud!

He received several awards and recognition during high school. He defied all the odds and graduated! He works a full-time job, helps around the house, and does everything that the doctor said he would never do. Things are still hard for him to process at times, but he never allows it to get him down. The road has been difficult but my God is truly awesome!

Chapter 5
THE POURING RAIN

A brisk chill brought Sabrina out of her trip down memory lane. She looked up to see that she was seated directly under a vent. *Figures,* she thought ruefully, but did not move. Although cold, Sabrina saw it as a blessing: she tended to perspire when nervous, and could feel the dampness on her palms despite the cool chill.

She began to wish she could call her mother and hear her calming voice. *Mom...* Sabrina thought wistfully, and her mind returned to the past...

***

Tests are meant to mold and expand. Knowing this, I must have been next in line for God to put His direct hands on the potter's wheel, because what I was about to face almost blew me away.

I began this season of growing in my faith with my mom being diagnosed with an aggressive form of cancer.

Cancer. It was back again.

I was devastated because my mother was my hero. She was my greatest supporter, my best friend, my confidant, my cheerleader, and my shero. We were inseparable. Mom had survived so much and never once lost her faith. So to see her now dying like this cut a large hole deep in my heart. It was so difficult to see someone so independent become so dependent upon everyone else for her day to day activities.

This season was one of the hardest of my life. Mom was my everything and I had to watch her waste away, a little at a time, day after day. She didn't deserve this, not one bit. I found myself almost emotionally destroyed. As mom lay dying in her hospital bed, one of the final things she said to me was, "Sister, no matter what, always remember that we serve a mighty God." Those words are forever etched into my heart. I found it so surreal: here she was taking her last breaths and still had the strength to encourage me and praise our God.

During this time, I was pregnant with my second son and I knew that mom was fighting hard to hold on to see him. I praise God, even to this day, that she was able to be with me at the hospital while I was giving birth. I prayed and prayed for mom to be able to see her second grandchild and God provided me with my heart's desire. She got to hold him and kiss him, and he got to hear her voice (even though he doesn't remember).

Unfortunately, mom passed the following month. I knew she was dying, but when she actually passed on, it felt like my entire world crumbled. I received Christ into my life in high school and was definitely a person of faith, but when mom passed, I became very angry with God and had a lot of bitterness in my heart.

My mom was 49 years young when she died. She was the glue that held our family together. She loved the Lord and was a committed Sunday School teacher. I couldn't understand why God chose her and not some of the other folks in our family because she was the best that we had. Didn't God know that I needed her? Didn't He care at all that I just had my second son and still needed a mother's support?

When my mom passed, I really didn't mourn because I had to be the strong one for the rest of my family. My younger brother came to live with us to finish high school. I felt like I always had to put on a happy face to keep him encouraged. I learned to mask my pain very well. My heart became very cold and hard, and I became very bitter. I would cry myself to sleep every night and put on my game face every day. I continued to go to church, but couldn't tell you what the sermon was. No one really understood my pain nor did they ask. They went on with their lives as if nothing happened, and this made me angrier with each passing day. Angry thoughts swirled through my head:

Who am I supposed to turn to now?

No one cares about me.

I lived in torment and began to have nightmares about the time when I was molested as kid. The devil actually told me that he was going to kill me and he almost did. BUT God!

In the midst of losing my mom, I felt myself on a downward spiral. My husband began to distance himself and we grew apart. I felt like he wasn't supportive through my grieving nor did he care. I thought these things, even knowing how close he was to my mother. I'd never felt so alone in my life. I felt abandoned, ashamed, and invisible. It was just me and my two boys with this big hole in my heart.

I had a good friend that I would call when things got really bad. I would cry and she usually listened. That was all the support I had except for Aunt Rachel who would pray with me. I was in a depression for six months and it was pure hell.

The nightmares grew more intense, but I still didn't tell anyone other than Marcus about my molestation. Not only did I lose my mom, but things got really ugly between me and my husband. We were two ships passing in the night and became more like roommates than a married couple. I was angry with him for not caring like how I thought he should have. I couldn't take it anymore so I decided to file for a legal separation. He refused to leave the house and my attorney advised me not to leave, so we were under the same roof during this chaos. It was extremely stressful.

I reached a point where I could no longer pray nor did I have the desire to. My bitterness knew no bounds. It began to take a toll on my body. I began to throw up blood. I was a mess. I hid my depression, sadness, and physical ailments from people because I felt like no one really cared. I cried myself to sleep every night for six straight months.

One night, God appeared to me in a dream and allowed me to see myself. In the dream I began to throw up maggots and God told me that I was filthy and was making Him sick! This was the turning point for me. I never wanted to disappoint God and the dream scared me a lot. I cried out to Him and He began to work on my heart. Healing was beginning to take place within me.

God was faithful, healing me from the inside out. He began to heal my mind and began to heal my marriage. The road to peace was difficult; I was still grieving the death of my mom. But God's love restored my mind and He gave me strength to press forward.

My road to healing and wholeness was not without tests and trials. I felt the full brunt of what it was to be completely healed. It wasn't that God sent a basket of healing, or snapped His fingers and healed every boo-boo. It was a process. Whenever I felt that I was making huge strides, another hammer would come down.

I faced personal bankruptcy.

I faced foreclosure on my home.

Our financial bind combined with the uncertainty of where we would live caused me to lose half of my hair.

I felt out of control and out of bounds.

And then my oldest brother.

It was totally unexpected. He died of a heart attack. It was ironic because he died of a broken heart while my heart was being repaired. I was devastated and thought I couldn't take anymore.

This was the season that I learned the truth about being tested and the importance of passing the test.

The devil continued to attack me through dreams about the molestation of my youth until one night I cried out to God to completely heal me from the molestation. And praise God, I haven't had another nightmare since. It was at this point that I realized that if I just trusted God with it, that it would be cared for. I was looking so hard for people to make me feel better when it was God who held the key to make me whole.

In the middle of foreclosure and heartache, my third son was born. It felt like a piece of my heart was filled up. The love of my son began to save me just a little more. His love was innocent and so pure. He didn't judge me for my past and didn't care what happened to me. He was my manifestation of grace in the midst of the storm.

As I grew, I was called into ministry to do the work of the Lord Jesus Christ. For so long I ran from my calling, but as I began to turn and accept what God has called me to do, I met major opposition. I was faced with people who believed that women should not speak or preach the word of the Lord. I was faced with vain imaginations and it began to sow seeds of rejection and fear. I had trust in what God said, but I couldn't help what I saw and what I heard. I knew that God called me so I did all that I could to push ahead. I began to think a lot about Esther who was in a position to represent her people despite how big the risk. The opposition seemed great, but I stood on what God spoke to me, about me, and for me. I felt isolated and alone during this time yet I trusted God and stood on His word. And as God does, He placed a scripture in my heart to refer to when things seemed impossible:

"For I know the thoughts that I think toward you, says the LORD, thoughts of peace and not of evil, to give you a future and a hope." (NKJV) **Jeremiah 29:11**

God is good!

Chapter 6
THE CALL

I continued to sit there staring at the roses and reminiscing about my life and all that I had gone through. At that moment, I realized that I was much stronger than I ever thought that I could be and had so much gratitude in my heart that I had survived so many storms. The tears started to flow down my face and I began to quickly try and gather myself before my name was called to Mr. Kelly's office.

"Come on Sabrina, get yourself together girl," is what I kept thinking and uttering under my breathe. Normally, I would have been impatient just sitting and waiting for what seemed like an eternity, but this time I was thankful for the extra minutes which allowed me to gather myself and mentally prepare for whatever discussion was about to take place. As I took another glance at the beautiful bouquet, peace continued to fill me and I knew that no matter what, I would be just fine.

Amy made her way over to where I was sitting and told me that Mr. Kelly was ready to see me. As she turned to walk away, she gave me another glance and smiled as if she was trying to give me a sign that today would be a good day for me.

I had never been to Mr. Kelly's office and didn't know what to expect. The only people who were allowed inside his office were his executive team; everyone else had to be invited.

Amy walked ahead of me and opened the door to Mr. Kelly's office. I made my way inside and stood there until he finished his phone conversation and acknowledged my presence. He stood from behind his desk and reached out his had to shake mine. He had to be at least 6'3" and had salt and pepper hair. In a very deep voice he said, "Good morning Sabrina, I am sorry to have kept you waiting for so long. I had an unexpected call that lasted much longer than what I had anticipated. Please have a seat and relax."

I sat there trying not to allow my nerves to become unraveled and anxiously waited to hear why Mr. Kelly wanted to see me. I glanced over to the right and noticed that his office had such a beautiful view of the river. Looking at the water was very calming. My mind settled, and Mr. Kelly began to speak.

"Sabrina, I have been following your performance and have been extremely impressed. Your drive, knowledge and dedication is remarkable, and I am honored to have you on my team. What is your favorite color?"

I sat there trying to take in all of what Mr. Kelly just said, trying to hold back my emotions, and still somehow utter in a hopefully calm tone, "Blue is my favorite color."

Only after I answered him do I wonder what my favorite color has to do with this conversation. It seemed a bit odd to me, but I wasn't about to question him.

Mr. Kelly continued to speak. "What do you prefer, Nissan or Honda?" This was really getting weird, but I responded, "Nissan."

He scribbled on a note pad with every response. I sat utterly still and wondered why I was in his office and why he was asking me these strange questions. "Sabrina, the board and I have reviewed all the applicants who applied for the Senior Account Manager position and feel that it is only fitting that we extend the offer to you. You possess the character and talent that we need, and we can't think of anyone else more deserving. The position comes with an annualized salary of $170,000.00, a 20% bonus and a Blue Nissan Maxima. Your office will be located on the 7th floor with a picturesque view of the river. You will have your own assistant and will be assigned a reserved parking spot on the ground level of the garage. Here is your formal offer. Please read over it carefully and sign it if you accept. Sabrina, my company is better because of people like you."

I was stunned.

Was this really happening?

Oh my goodness, I can't believe what I am hearing!

The years of staying late working long hours, the times I felt that my efforts had gone unnoticed, they had finally paid off in a huge way! Tears began to well up in my eyes again because my dreams were becoming a reality. I sat and read over the offer and was still astonished at the goodness of God and all His blessings.

I signed the offer and handed it back to Mr. Kelly. He made me a copy, stood up and handed me the keys to my office. My eyes were now burning with tears and I was trying really hard not to cry. My heart was so full of gratitude. Mr. Kelly escorted me to the elevator and as the door opened, he shook my hand and congratulated me on a job well done.

I stepped inside the elevator and lost it. The tears flowed and all I could think about was how momma was right: God always takes care of His own and His plan is bigger than anything that we could ever dream.

At that moment, I realized that everything that I had experienced in life was instrumental in me becoming who I was. Every season had its assigned purpose, and what should have destroyed me only made me stronger. I was once so broken I didn't think I could be repaired, but God's love restored me, renewed my will to persevere and to dream again.

I thought again about my life, and realized that it was not a project to be repaired. Rather, I am a rose that was destined to bloom again and again through God's grace and mercy.

GRATEFUL is who I am. Blooming again and walking with confidence. This withered rose has bloomed AGAIN!

CLINTORIA SESSION

Chapter 7

WORDS TO LIVE BY

Beloved,

God loves you, always and in all ways. He knows your heart's deepest desires, and has bestowed upon all of us His holy and precious word. The next few pages include my favorite scriptures that have helped me during trials and challenges in life, and I pray they bring you great comfort as well.

Peace be unto you,
Clintoria Session

***

When Experiencing Fear

II Timothy 1:7
"For God hath not given us the spirit of fear; but of power, and of love, and a sound mind."

I John 4:18
"There is no fear in love; but perfect love casteth out fear; because fear hath torment. He that feareth is not made perfect in love."

Psalms 91:4-7
"He shall cover thee with his feathers, and under his wings shalt thou trust; his truth shall be thy shield and buckler. Thou shalt not be afraid for the terror by night, nor the arrow that flieth by day; nor for the pestilence that walketh in darkness; nor for the destruction that wasteth at noonday. A thousand shall fall at thy side, and ten thousand at thy right hand; but it shall not come nigh thee."

John 14:27
"Peace I leave with you, my peace I give unto you: not as the world giveth, give I unto you. Let not your heart be troubled, neither let it be afraid."

Reflections

When You Lack Confidence

Philippians 4:13
"I can do all things through Christ which strengthens me."

Romans 8:37
"Nay, in all these things we are more than conquerors through him that loved us."

I John 5:14-15
"And this is the confidence that we have in him, that, if we ask anything according to his will, he heareth us; and if we know that he hear us, whatsoever we ask, we know that we have the petitions that we desired of him."

II Corinthians 7:16
"I rejoice therefore that I have confidence in you in all things."

Reflections

Forgiving Others

Mathew 6: 14-15
"For if ye forgive men their trespasses, your heavenly Father will also forgive you; but if you forgive not men their trespasses, neither will your Father forgive your trespasses."

Colossians 3:13
"Forbearing one another, and forgiving one another, if any man have a quarrel against any: even as Christ forgave you, so also do ye."

Romans 12:21
"Be not overcome of evil, but overcome evil with good."

Ephesians 4:31-32
"Let all bitterness, and wrath, and anger, and clamor, and evil speaking, be put away from you, with all malice: and be ye kind one to another, tender-hearted, forgiving one another, even as God for Christ's sake hath forgiven you."

Reflections

In Need of Peace

Isaiah 26:3
"Thou wilt keep him in perfect peace, whose mind is stayed on thee: because he trusted in thee."

John 14:27
"Peace, I leave with you, my peace I give unto you; not as the world giveth, give I unto you. Let not your heart be troubled, neither let it be afraid."

Philippians 4:6-7
"Be careful for nothing; but in everything by prayer and supplication with thanksgiving let your requests be made known unto God. And the peace of God, which passeth all understanding, shall keep your hearts and minds through Christ Jesus."

Psalm 37:11
"But the meek shall inherit the earth; and shall delight themselves in the abundance of peace."

Reflections

In Need of Strength

Isaiah 40:29
"He giveth power to the faint; and to them that have no might he increaseth strength."

Psalm 18:2
"The Lord is my rock, and my fortress, and my deliverer; my God, my strength, in whom I will trust; my buckler, and the horn of my salvation, and my high tower."

Ephesians 6:13
"Wherefore take unto you the whole armor of God, that ye may be able to withstand in the evil day, and having done all, to stand."

Isaiah 40:31
"But they that wait upon the Lord shall renew their strength; they shall mount up with wings as eagles; they shall run, and not be weary; and they shall walk, and not faint."

Reflections

ABOUT THE AUTHOR

Clintoria Wakefield Session is an energetic, caring and dedicated Human Resources professional with over 20 years of experience helping people break barriers to live their best lives. Clintoria is certified to facilitate, speak, train and coach in the areas of leadership development, personal development and career development. She is also the CEO of Coach Tori Empowers equipping others to excel both personally and professionally.

A native of Seneca, SC, she and her husband, Samuel Session, Jr., have been married for 24 years and have three extraordinary sons.

Made in the USA
Columbia, SC
25 February 2019